31 DAYS OF HEARING GOD SPEAK

31 DAYS OF HEARING GOD SPEAK

How Listening To God Speak Can Change Your Life

HERB COTTON

ELITE

Xulon Press Elite
2301 Lucien Way #415
Maitland, FL 32751
407.339.4217
www.xulonpress.com

© 2017 by Herb Cotton

Edited by Xulon Press.

All rights reserved solely by the author. The author guarantees all contents are original and do not infringe upon the legal rights of any other person or work. No part of this book may be reproduced in any form without the permission of the author. The views expressed in this book are not necessarily those of the publisher.

Unless otherwise indicated, Scripture quotations taken from the Amplified Bible (AMP). Copyright © 1954, 1958, 1962, 1964, 1965, 1987 by The Lockman Foundation. Used by permission. All rights reserved.

Scripture quotations taken from the English Standard Version (ESV). Copyright © 2001 by Crossway, a publishing ministry of Good News Publishers. Used by permission. All rights reserved.

Scripture quotations taken from the King James Version (KJV) – *public domain.*

Scripture quotations taken from the Holy Bible, New International Version (NIV). Copyright © 1973, 1978, 1984, 2011 by Biblica, Inc.™. Used by permission. All rights reserved.

Scripture quotations taken from the New King James Version (NKJV). Copyright © 1982 by Thomas Nelson, Inc. Used by permission. All rights reserved.

Scripture quotations taken from the Holy Bible, New Living Translation (NLT). Copyright ©1996, 2004, 2007 by Tyndale House Foundation. Used by permission of Tyndale House Publishers, Inc.

Printed in the United States of America.

ISBN-13: 9781545620045

Table of Contents

1	The Foundation for Life	1
2	The Source of Life	3
3	Have You Been Born Twice?	5
4	Has Your Sin Debt Been Settled?	7
5	Stewardship of Time	9
6	What Is the Hope for Dying Relationships?	11
7	How to Have Confidence in Your Life	13
8	Why Do You Lack Anything?	15
9	The Gift of Faith	17
10	The Gift of Hope	19
11	The Gift of Love	20
12	The Gift of Forgiveness	22
13	Prayer	24
14	Anxiety	25
15	Family	27
16	Courage	29
17	Confidence	31
18	Consecration	33
19	Trials and Troubles	34
20	Abide	36
21	God's Presence	38
22	What It Means to Be Chosen	40
23	Are You Being Transformed?	42
24	What Is God's Standard for His People?	44
25	How Can I Ever Meet the Standard to Be Perfect?	45
26	Be Kind	47
27	Be Thankful	49
28	Be Humble	51
29	The Responsibility of the Hearer of the Word of God	52
30	The Word of God	54
31	Prayer Is the Lifeblood of the Body of Christ	56

Dedication

I dedicate this book to the memory of my mother,
Virginia "Bertha" Watts.

Foreword

Herb Cotton is a lifelong servant of our Lord Jesus Christ. As a pastor, host of radio ministry, Praying for You, and a partner in the Alaska Governors Prayer Breakfast program, these foundations of Herb's service to the Christian community and his love for Jesus comes alive in his book.

Thirty-One Days of Hearing God Speak is for anyone who will simply do His glorious will. Jesus said in Matthew 12:50, "Whosoever shall do the will of my Father which is in heaven; the same is my brother, and sister and mother."

The Word of God reveals its substance by personal study. This book requires the believer to meditate on God's Word and concentrate to hear what the Word reveals to your heart.

Meditation produces revelation truth. Revelation truth is always Bible proven, and this makes way for God's nature to be alive in the soul of the believer.

As one's heart is prepared to receive the manifested blessings from the Word of God, we learn that we have a heart that hears and brings results.

This book is a wonderful presentation to encourage the reader to live a life that is increasingly exciting to glorify God increasingly day by day.

Thirty-One Days of Hearing God Speak will speak to your heart. So meditate (ignite), revelate (effect), and manifestate (results) to the glory of God. This book is a must-read.

Ray Dahl

Introduction

Why another book of daily devotionals? Well, this book is more than that. It is the story of my life. However, it is not about me, but is about my God and the Bible.

I wrote thirty-one daily devotionals for this book. I drew upon the four seasons of my life. I used football as an analogy. I am seventy-six years old. I'm in the fourth quarter myself, and my goal is to finish the race and win the prize.

First Quarter:	Birth–25 years
Second Quarter:	26 years–50 years
Third Quarter:	51 years – 75years
Fourth Quarter:	76+ years

The Bible has been my companion in every season of my life. I grew up in the church. At an early age, I received training in an organization called BYPU. The longhand for that is Baptist Young Peoples Union. Later, it was changed to the Baptist Training Union. The church realized that not just young people needed training in Christian education, but rather the whole congregation.

In selecting the thirty-one chapters that make up this book, I drew from lessons I learned in all of the seasons of my life. I am indebted to many pastors, teachers, and others who have contributed to my spiritual growth.

My goal in writing this book is to leave a legacy for my children, grandchildren, great-grandchildren, family, and friends.

My dream is to use the book as a platform for completing my purpose for the remainder of my life using the spiritual gifts that the Lord has given me.

I have come this far in my life by having faith in God, and I am too close to heaven to turn around now.

I am driven and encouraged by the members of my family, some of whom have completed their earthly journey, who had this motto in their lives: "If I can help somebody as I travel on, then my living has not been in vain."

I have been young, but now I am old. However, I feel like a young man. I have discovered that it pays richly to listen when God speaks. The important thing is to keep moving forward. For me, it has been a life of walking in the footsteps of Jesus.

My prayer for you, as you read the words in this book, is that God would use His words and my words to encourage and edify your life.

Proverbs 16:24 (KJV)

"Pleasant words *are as* a honeycomb, sweet to the soul, and health to the bones."

1
The Foundation for Life

God Speaks
1 Corinthians 13:13 (NKJV)
"And now abide faith, hope, love, these three; but the greatest of these *is* love."

Listen
Is it the desire of your heart to live a life of purpose, and to leave a meaningful legacy for those who follow you?

One of my favorite chapters of the Bible is 1 Corinthians 13. However, I like to begin the reading at the last verse of the previous chapter.

1 Corinthians 12:31 (NKJV)
"But earnestly desire the best gifts. And yet I show you a more excellent way."

To live the best life, Paul speaks about the gift of love, which is the greatest of all. Paul gives fifteen attributes of love.

> **1 Corinthians 13:4-7 (NKJV)** Love suffers long *and* is kind; love does not envy; love does not parade itself, is not puffed up; does not behave rudely, does not seek its own, is not provoked, thinks no evil; does not rejoice in iniquity, but rejoices in the truth; bears all things, believes all things, hopes all things, endures all things.

To live the way of life that is best of all, we must build on the best foundation. Are you constructing your life on the three things that will last forever? Remember, the greatest of these is love.

1 John 4:7-8 (NKJV)
"Beloved, let us love one another, for love is of God; and everyone who loves is born of God and knows God. He who does not love does not know God, for God is love."

Prayer
Father, I pray You would grant to each of us a burning desire to build our life in God, and upon God, who is love.

2
The Source of Life

God Speaks
John 14:6 (KJV)
"Jesus saith unto him, I am the way, the truth, and the life: no man cometh unto the Father, but by me."

Listen
Who is Jesus?
John 1:1-3 (KJV)
"In the beginning was the Word, and the Word was with God, and the Word was God. The same was in the beginning with God. All things were made by him; and without him was not any thing made that was made."

This pre-existent Jesus became flesh and lived among humanity.
John 1:14 (KJV)
"And the Word was made flesh, and dwelt among us, (and we beheld his glory, the glory as of the only begotten of the Father,) full of grace and truth."

Why did Jesus become human flesh?
John 3:16 (KJV)
"For God so loved the world, that he gave his only begotten Son, that whosoever believeth in him should not perish, but have everlasting life."

The most profound truth is a simple truth. I have briefly shared with you the gospel of Christ. This God-spoken truth is a solemn and sacred business. The stakes are high; it's a matter of life and death.

Romans 3:22-23 (NLT)
"We are made right with God by placing our faith in Jesus Christ. And this is true for everyone who believes, no matter who we are. For everyone has sinned; we all fall short of God's glorious standard."

Romans 6:23 (NLT)
"For the wages of sin is death, but the free gift of God is eternal life through Christ Jesus our Lord."

Romans 5:8 (NLT)
"But God showed his great love for us by sending Christ to die for us while we were still sinners."

Romans 10:9-10 (NLT)
"If you confess with your mouth that Jesus is Lord and believe in your heart that God raised him from the dead, you will be saved. For it is by believing in your heart that you are made right with God, and it is by confessing with your mouth that you are saved."

Romans 10:13 (NLT)
"For everyone who calls on the name of the Lord will be saved."

John 1:12-13 (KJV)
"But as many as received him, to them gave he power to become the sons of God, *even* to them that believe on his name: which were born, not of blood, nor of the will of the flesh, nor of the will of man, but of God."

Prayer
Father, I pray everyone who hears and receives this word will acknowledge that they are a sinner, and need a Savior. Father, I pray any who have not received Jesus will receive Him today. Father, I pray those who have accepted Jesus will share the good news with someone who has not.

3
Have You Been Born Twice?

God Speaks
John 3:1-3 (KJV)
"There was a man of the Pharisees, named Nicodemus, a ruler of the Jews: The same came to Jesus by night, and said unto him, Rabbi, we know that thou art a teacher come from God: for no man can do these miracles that thou doest, except God be with him. Jesus answered and said unto him, Verily, verily, I say unto thee, except a man be born again, he cannot see the kingdom of God."

Listen
It is not your education, wealth, or position that enables you to understand the mysteries of life and understand the means of access to God. Nicodemus came to the right source to get the right answer about how to gain access to the Kingdom of God.

God, in Christ, is the source of eternal life. The truth is revealed in the conversation Nicodemus had with Jesus. I recommend you read the entire book of John. The reason for reading the Gospel of John is described in the following verse.

John 20:31 (KJV)
"But these are written, that ye might believe that Jesus is the Christ, the Son of God; and that believing ye might have life through his name."

Prayer
Father God, my heart aches for the hearts and souls of those who have only been born once. Father, I pray everyone who hears this word will believe it and receive it. Father, I thank you for sending Jesus to die once for us so that we would not have to die twice.

2 Corinthians 5:21 (KJV)
"For he hath made him *to be* sin for us, who knew no sin; that we might be made the righteousness of God in him."

4
Has Your Sin Debt Been Settled?

God Speaks
Romans 6:6 (KJV)
"Knowing this, that our old man is crucified with *him*, that the body of sin might be destroyed, that henceforth we should not serve sin."

Listen
Do you know your old sinful self was crucified with Christ when He died on the cross? Can you categorically say what the Apostle Paul said in his letter to the church at Galatia?

Galatians 2:20 (KJV)
"I am crucified with Christ: nevertheless I live; yet not I, but Christ liveth in me: and the life which I now live in the flesh I live by the faith of the Son of God, who loved me, and gave himself for me."

If this is your testimony, you are in a safe and glorious place in your life. You can say with your words and your manner of living what Paul wrote in the following verse.

Romans 8:1 (KJV)
"*There is* therefore now no condemnation to them which are in Christ Jesus, who walk not after the flesh, but after the Spirit."

How then will you live? Look back at Galatians 2:20 and be grounded; look forward to this wonderful word and be encouraged.

Romans 6:13 (KJV)
"Neither yield ye your members *as* instruments of unrighteousness unto sin: but yield yourselves unto God, as those that are alive from the dead, and your members *as* instruments of righteousness unto God."

Sin is no longer your master. You have a new owner. You serve Jesus and He lives in you. Therefore, you are never alone. In Christ, you have the power to say no to temptation. Jesus is the truth, you know the truth, and the truth lives in you.

So, the reality is this: you know the truth and you have the power to stand in the truth. The Father speaks to you, Jesus lives in you, and the Holy Spirit is God's gift to you to tutor and give you strength. God is in you, God is with you, and God is for you.

1 Corinthians 10:12-13 (KJV)
"Wherefore let him that thinketh he standeth take heed lest he fall. There hath no temptation taken you but such as is common to man: but God *is* faithful, who will not suffer you to be tempted above that ye are able; but will with the temptation also make a way to escape, that ye may be able to bear *it*."

Prayer
Father God, we thank you from the depths of our heart for the provisions, protection, and power You give to Your children.

Father, I pray we will always remember the truth of our Christ, and not the conditions or the circumstances in our environment.

To our great and generous God, we will always be grateful for your supernatural grace, tender mercies, and unfailing love.

5
Stewardship of Time

God Speaks
Ephesians 5:15-17 (KJV)
"See then that ye walk circumspectly, not as fools, but as wise, redeeming the time, because the days are evil. Wherefore be ye not unwise, but understanding what the will of the Lord *is*."

Listening
When we think about stewardship, we think of time, talent, and treasure. In the case of time, we all have the same amount. We all have 168 hours in the week. I like to manage my use of time by the week. We don't all have the same amount of talent and treasure.

I have found in life, business, and ministry that you cannot manage time. You can't save time. You can spend it and invest it.

How can we be good stewards of time? The Bible gives us three principles:

1. Live wisely.
2. Live in the present.
3. Live in the will of God.

We can use time, and we should use it wisely. I have found these three truths to be helpful in managing my life as I seek to invest the time I have in the God-provided opportunities I have each week.

1. Time is perishable.

Psalm 90:12 (KJV)
"So teach *us* to number our days, that we may apply *our* hearts unto wisdom."

2. Practice making the main thing the main thing.
Matthew 6:33 (KJV)
"But seek ye first the kingdom of God, and his righteousness; and all these things shall be added unto you."

3. Never give up.

Galatians 6:9 (KJV)
"And let us not be weary in well doing: for in due season we shall reap, if we faint not."

Prayer
Father God, help us, by the strength You provide, to live wisely, live in the present, and live in the will of God by the wisdom and power of God.

6
What Is the Hope for Dying Relationships?

God Speaks
Philippians 4:4-5 (KJV)
"Rejoice in the Lord always: *and* again I say, Rejoice. Let your moderation be known unto all men. The Lord *is* at hand."

Listen
It pays to listen to the voice of God when you read the Word of God. One of the burdens on my heart, and it has been there for a considerable amount of time, is the destruction of relationships in our society.

The word that leaped off the page and into my heart when I read the passage above is the word "rejoice."

As I meditated upon that word, the Spirit of God spoke to me and revealed to me that there is hope for dying relationships. What did I see that gave me hope?

This is what I saw and what I heard with the eyes and ears of my heart. This is not from me, but from the Lord.

When you rejoice in the Lord always, you don't have time to complain about the faults and business of other people. There is nothing more destructive to relationships than complaining and gossiping.

There is an incredible promise found in the Bible that I believe can transform the world as we know it. Notice the four things that are in the following passage. If we do these things, God will heal our broken relationships and our world.

2 Chronicles 7:14 (KJV)
"If my people, which are called by my name, shall humble themselves, and pray, and seek my face, and turn from their wicked ways;

then will I hear from heaven, and will forgive their sin, and will heal their land."

When God calls His people to do something, He always gives them the gifts to carry out His commands. We have within us the power to have an amazing relationship with God, and with others. Are you using the gifts God has given you in abundance?

Galatians 5:22-23 (KJV)
"But the fruit of the Spirit is love, joy, peace, longsuffering, gentleness, goodness, faith,
Meekness, temperance: against such there is no law."

Prayer
Father God, thank you for being so gracious to us. Father, give us a burning desire and the faith to work out the fruit of the Holy Spirit which you have produced in the life of Your people who walk in the Spirit of God.

Galatians 5:16 (KJV)
"*This* I say then, walk in the Spirit, and ye shall not fulfil the lust of the flesh."

7
How to Have Confidence in Your Life

God Speaks
Psalm 55:4-7 (KJV)
"My heart is sore pained within me: and the terrors of death are fallen upon me.
Fearfulness and trembling are come upon me, and horror hath overwhelmed me.
And I said, Oh that I had wings like a dove! *for then* would I fly away, and be at rest.
Lo, *then* would I wander far off, *and* remain in the wilderness. Selah."

Listen
Why are we so fearful? Fear that grips our hearts and debilitates our lives is not from God. Listen to what God has to say about this kind of fear.

2 Timothy 1:7 (KJV)
"For God hath not given us the spirit of fear; but of power, and of love, and of a sound mind."
How can you activate the gifts of power, love, and self-discipline which God has so freely and generously given to you?

When fear knocks on your door, don't open it. Turn to God and find rest and renewal in Him.

Psalm 46:1-2 (KJV)
"God *is* our refuge and strength, a very present help in trouble.
Therefore will not we fear, though the earth be removed, and though the mountains be carried into the midst of the sea;"

When you open the door of your heart and give the Lord your whole heart, you will experience transformational change. You will be able to joyfully sing this old hymn of the faithful written by Rufus McDonald in 1914.

"I'm possessed of a hope, that is steadfast and sure,
Since Jesus came into my heart;
And no dark clouds of doubt now my pathway obscure,
Since Jesus came into my heart."

Prayer

Father God, we are grateful for Your giving us sufficient faith to overcome all of our problems. Father, our confidence comes from allowing You to be our refuge and our strength.

8
Why Do You Lack Anything?

God Speaks
Psalm 27:1 (KJV)
"The LORD *is* my light and my salvation; whom shall I fear? The LORD *is* the strength of my life; of whom shall I be afraid?"

Listen
If you heard from a source that was inexhaustible, and that source was willing to provide for all of your needs, would you be interested?

Consider what David says in just one verse of this Psalm of praise and thanksgiving to God.

"The Lord is my light.
The Lord is my salvation.
The Lord is my fortress."

David concluded he had nothing to fear. Then, he goes further and makes this declaration about the provisions of the Lord.

Psalm 27:3 (KJV)
"Though a host should encamp against me, my heart shall not fear: though war should rise against me, in this *will* I *be* confident."

There was a dear woman of God whom I served with in Alaska for many years who touched me deeply when she would sing this song by Bill and Gloria Gaither.

"Every need He is supplying,
Plenteous grace He bestows.
Every day my way gets brighter,
The longer I serve Him, the sweeter He grows."

The Apostle Paul wrote the following encouraging words to the church at Rome.

Romans 8:31 (KJV)
"What shall we then say to these things? If God *be* for us, who *can be* against us?"
Why not accept this invitation?

Psalm 55:22 (KJV)
"Cast thy burden upon the LORD, and he shall sustain thee: he shall never suffer the righteous to be moved."

Prayer
Father God, thank you for being a loving, heavenly Father in whom we can look to and lean upon for all of our needs. Father, thank you for an abundance of love, grace, and mercy which you have freely given to us and which we gratefully receive with our whole heart.

9
The Gift of Faith

God Speaks
Ephesians 2:8-9 (KJV)
"For by grace are ye saved through faith; and that not of yourselves: *it is* the gift of God:
Not of works, lest any man should boast."

Listen
I never shall forget the day I experienced God's grace and, by faith, received Jesus into my heart. It was December 31, 1949.

The day I received Jesus into my heart was the best day of my life. I was a nine-year-old boy who did not have a testimony. But, through the words the pastor spoke that night, and the words of the hymn, "Pass Me Not O, Gentle Savior," I was born from above.

Let's look into the Word of God to learn more about faith. Notice what the Bible says about the how and where of faith.

Romans 10:17 (KJV)
"So then faith *cometh* by hearing, and hearing by the word of God."

Also, notice how the Bible defines faith.

Hebrews 11:1 (AMP)
"Now faith is the assurance (the confirmation, the title deed) of the things [we] hope for, being the proof of things [we] do not see and the conviction of their reality [faith perceiving as real fact what is not revealed to the senses]."

When you have faith in God, you get what God can do.

Luke 1:37 (KJV)
"For with God nothing shall be impossible."

When you have God living in your heart, occupying every room of your life, you have the promise you will never be alone.

Hebrews 13:5 (NKJV)

"*Let your* conduct *be* without covetousness; *be* content with such things as you have. For He Himself has said, *"I will never leave you nor forsake you."*"

It's not about how much money you have. Rather, it's about how much of the Master you have. Give Him all of you, and in exchange, He will give you all of Himself.

Prayer

Father God, with thanksgiving in our hearts and on our lips, we surrender our will to Thy will. Father, You are the giver and we are the receiver. Lord, give us sufficient faith to do Your will.

10
The Gift of Hope

God Speaks
Romans 15:13 (NKJV)
"Now may the God of hope fill you with all joy and peace in believing, that you may abound in hope by the power of the Holy Spirit."

Listen
One thing I have come to appreciate over the course of my walk with the Lord is the importance of having hope. I am so grateful that hope lasts forever. Let these words of God richly encourage you and give you a hope that will never run out.

Jeremiah 29:11 (KJV)
"For I know the thoughts that I think toward you, saith the LORD, thoughts of peace, and not of evil, to give you an expected end."

Isaiah 40:31 (KJV)
"But they that wait upon the LORD shall renew *their* strength; they shall mount up with wings as eagles; they shall run, and not be weary; *and* they shall walk, and not faint."

Psalm 39:7 (KJV)
"And now, Lord, what wait I for? My hope *is* in thee."

Prayer
Father God, we say from the depths of our hearts, thank you, Lord, for giving us the things we need the most, and that will last forever.

11
The Gift of Love

God Speaks
Psalm 147:11 (KJV)
"The LORD taketh pleasure in them that fear him, in those that hope in his mercy."

Listen
I am growing in the process of paying attention to God when He speaks and being who He wants me to be. I greatly desire to be the person He made me to be. I am not a perfect man because I have a human father. Jesus, the God Man, is the only man who was perfect because His father was God.

Luke 1:34-35 (NKJV)
"Then Mary said to the angel, "How can this be, since I do not know a man?"
And the angel answered and said to her, "*The* Holy Spirit will come upon you, and the power of the Highest will overshadow you; therefore, also, that Holy One who is to be born will be called the Son of God.""

How great and wonderful is this God? He is Sovereign; He reigns on high, but condescends and looks low. Have you had the experience of hearing God's call to come to Him? Have you received His gift of love?

Romans 5:5 (NKJV)
"Now hope does not disappoint, because the love of God has been poured out in our hearts by the Holy Spirit who was given to us."

What is the key that opens the door of your heart to allow God to come into it and live there forever?

John 1:12-13 (KJV)
"But as many as received him, to them gave he power to become the sons of God, *even* to them that believe on his name:
Which were born, not of blood, nor of the will of the flesh, nor of the will of man, but of God."

Can you say that the blessed assurance of Jesus is yours? God's presence in your life is just one step of faith away. Why not take it now?

John 3:16 (KJV)
"For God so loved the world, that he gave his only begotten Son, that whosoever believeth in him should not perish, but have everlasting life."

Prayer
Father God, we thank you for loving us first. We are so grateful that You have poured out Your love into our hearts.

12
The Gift of Forgiveness

God Speaks
Mark 11:25 (KJV)
"And when ye stand praying, forgive, if ye have ought against any: that your Father also which is in heaven may forgive you your trespasses."

Listen
I am completely aware that I am not a perfect person. I can't count all the times I have missed the mark when it comes to knowing and doing the will of God.

Oh, I shudder to think where I would be if it were not for the love of God that has been poured out into my heart by the Holy Spirit that He has given me.

The Bible is so central in my life because no one could do for me what the God of the Bible did for me. It is the God of the Bible who provided the means for my salvation. I owe everything to Jesus. If our troubled world needs anything, it needs Jesus.

I am so glad that I can sing from the depths of my heart, "Now I belong to Jesus, and Jesus belongs to me."

What can I do in response to all that God has done for me? I can do what He commands me to do; I can love and forgive others. I remember a preacher saying, "God commands you to love me, and you can't love me without forgiving me."

John 13:34 (KJV)
"A new commandment I give unto you, That ye love one another; as I have loved you, that ye also love one another."

Prayer
Father God, we thank you continually for your amazing grace and tender mercies. Father, forgive us our debts as we forgive our debtors. Father, help us to never decouple love and forgiveness.

13
Prayer

God Speaks
1 Thessalonians 5:17 (KJV)
"Pray without ceasing."

Listen
Do you believe you should breathe continually? That is what God's Word is telling us to do. If God is present in you, why would you ever want to stop talking to Him? Jesus said in Hebrews 13:5b, "... I will never leave you nor forsake you." Why would you ever decide to stop praying? Let's make prayer as normal as breathing. Believers who are alive should never stop praying.

Luke 18:1 (KJV)
"And he spake a parable unto them *to this end*, that men ought always to pray, and not to faint;"

Life in this world will take you on journeys that result in mountain-top experiences. However, most of life happens in the valley. In the valley, we have joys and sorrows.

We cannot control all of the circumstances of our lives, but we can stay in communion, and in connection, with our God.

Colossians 4:2 (KJV)
"Continue in prayer, and watch in the same with thanksgiving;"

Prayer
Father God, we are so thankful for the prayer Jesus gave to His first followers. Father, may we all be people of prayer.

14
Anxiety

God Speaks
Philippians 4:6-8 (KJV)
"Be careful for nothing; but in every thing by prayer and supplication with thanksgiving let your requests be made known unto God.
And the peace of God, which passeth all understanding, shall keep your hearts and minds through Christ Jesus.
Finally, brethren, whatsoever things are true, whatsoever things *are* honest, whatsoever things *are* just, whatsoever things *are* pure, whatsoever things *are* lovely, whatsoever things *are* of good report; if *there be* any virtue, and if *there be* any praise, think on these things."

Listen
The admonishment here is clear. The recipients were told, "Pray about everything." When we face anxiety, we are told, "Don't worry about anything."

I have often heard it said, if you are going to worry, don't pray; and if you are going to pray, don't worry. The solution is to pray first and put your worries in God's hands.

Even when we know the message of truth, it is still difficult to follow when the moment arrives that results in anxiety or worry. When we are anxious, it is often hard to put a finger on the source. However, when we worry, we can often name the problem. When we have anxiety, worry, and are fretting, we are not acting in the character of being a child of God. Our troubles often revolve around people, things, or situations.

Consider these three ways to which we could respond to our anxiety and worry.

1. We insist on having things our way: Fight.
2. If we can't have our way, we take the highway: Flight.
3. We say like Jesus, "Not my way, but Thy way": Talk to God.

When we take everything to God, the anxiety will flee in the presence of God, and the peace of God will rule and reign in our lives.
Our problems and struggles will come and go, but God will never leave us or forsake us. He will give us His peace, and no power can take it from us.

John 14:1 (KJV)
"Let not your heart be troubled: ye believe in God, believe also in me."

John 14:27 (KJV)
"Peace I leave with you, my peace I give unto you: not as the world giveth, give I unto you. Let not your heart be troubled, neither let it be afraid."

Prayer
Father God, we are so grateful that we don't have to carry the burdens of anxiety and worry on our shoulders alone.

15
Family

God Speaks
Romans 8:15-16 (KJV)
"For ye have not received the spirit of bondage again to fear; but ye have received the Spirit of adoption, whereby we cry, Abba, Father. The Spirit itself beareth witness with our spirit, that we are the children of God:"

Listen
There is nothing more precious than family. I am a father and a grandfather, and my children, grandchildren, and great-grandchildren are always welcome to come home to Papa.

Even if your earthly father and mother forsake you, if you are a child of God, you can always come to your Heavenly Father. In fact, the presence of God in your life is forever because Jesus said He would never leave you nor forsake you.

In the following passage, Jesus speaks of His promise to always be present in the lives of His people.

John 14:15-20 (KJV)
"If ye love me, keep my commandments.
And I will pray the Father, and he shall give you another Comforter, that he may abide with you for ever;
Even the Spirit of truth; whom the world cannot receive, because it seeth him not, neither knoweth him: but ye know him; for he dwelleth with you, and shall be in you.
I will not leave you comfortless: I will come to you.
Yet a little while, and the world seeth me no more; but ye see me: because I live, ye shall live also.
At that day ye shall know that I *am* in my Father, and ye in me, and I in you."

Prayer
Father God, we are so thankful for the value You place on family. Oh, the blessing of being able to call You, "Abba, Father."

16
Courage

God Speaks
Psalm 31:24 (KJV)
"Be of good courage, and he shall strengthen your heart, all ye that hope in the LORD."

Listen
Do you have an unmet need for courage in your life? If you do, what is your source? I remember a message I heard by Billy Graham in the 1980s that has greatly informed my understanding of where to find courage. Billy Graham spoke of his discipline of reading five Psalms for encouragement and one Proverb for wisdom each day.

In Psalm 31, David said strength and courage come from putting your hope in the Lord.

Why should you put your hope in the Lord? I invite you to listen and hear the Word of God.

Isaiah 40:10 (KJV)
"Behold, the Lord GOD will come with strong *hand*, and his arm shall rule for him: behold, his reward *is* with him, and his work before him."

If you were to take an inventory of your most pressing needs, what would you include? Why not stop right now and make a list by writing down whatever is on your mind without evaluating the value of it. You will be surprised what will come after you write the first thing down.

If you need strength and courage, God is able and willing to give it to you. God will provide you everything that you need to fulfill the purpose for which He made you. If you trust in God, you can rely on Him to do His part.

Philippians 4:19 (KJV)
"But my God shall supply all your need according to his riches in glory by Christ Jesus."

The Sovereign Lord is able and willing to take your cares and give you courage. Hear His invitation and heed it; you will be strong and courageous.

1 Peter 5:7 (KJV)
"Casting all your care upon him; for he careth for you."

Prayer
Father God, Sovereign Lord, we are so thankful for the courage and hope we have because of our position of being in Christ.

Father, no one needs to be left behind because the door of deliverance is available, and the season of grace is open to all who come to Jesus.

John 10:9 (KJV)
"I am the door: by me if any man enter in, he shall be saved, and shall go in and out, and find pasture."

17
Confidence

God Speaks
Romans 8:25 (KJV)
"But if we hope for that we see not, *then* do we with patience wait for *it*."

Listen
Do you have hopes and dreams for things you do not see? When you are in the will of God, nothing is impossible. It takes practice and patience. It also takes faith in God.

Hebrews 11:1 (AMP)
"Now faith is the assurance (the confirmation, the title deed) of the things [we] hope for, being the proof of things [we] do not see and the conviction of their reality [faith perceiving as real fact what is not revealed to the senses]."

Hope in God is possible through the eyes of the heart. The way to have hope, and to access the power that is within you, is to have the Holy Spirit of God living in your heart. The Holy Spirit is God's gift to His children.

Romans 5:5 (NKJV)
"Now hope does not disappoint, because the love of God has been poured out in our hearts by the Holy Spirit who was given to us."

To make your hopes and dreams become a reality, put your trust in God, who can do anything but fail, and who will never disappoint you. Take the first step; it can be a small step, but make it a step forward, a step toward Jesus.

"Footprints of Jesus,
That makes the pathway glow;
We will follow the steps of Jesus
Where'er they go."
Author: MBB.Slade (1871)

Proverbs 16:9 (KJV)
"A man's heart deviseth his way: but the LORD directeth his steps."

Prayer
Father God, thank you for the faith we have in You; that we can trust You with our whole heart, and with the confidence that You will never let us down.

1 John 5:14-15 (KJV)
"And this is the confidence that we have in him, that, if we ask any thing according to his will, he heareth us:
And if we know that he hear us, whatsoever we ask, we know that we have the petitions that we desired of him."

18
Consecration

God Speaks
2 Corinthians 13:11 (KJV)
"Finally, brethren, farewell. Be perfect, be of good comfort, be of one mind, live in peace; and the God of love and peace shall be with you."

Listen
The above verse speaks to God's children; the set apart ones, the saints. Are you in that number? If not, do you want to be a member of the family of God?

The lyrics of this hymn , "Draw Me Nearer" express the prayer of my heart.

"Consecrate me now to Thy service, Lord,
By the power of grace divine;
Let my soul look up with a steadfast hope,
And my will be lost in Thine."

The four Be's in the key verse are the character traits of the saints of the ages that I desire to be—the character traits that others would see reflected in my life.

Be mature.
Be encouraged.
Be of the same mind with one another.
Be at peace.

Prayer
Father God, we pray You would consecrate us to the service of the coming of Thy kingdom and will to be done on earth as it is in heaven.

19
Trials and Troubles

God Speaks
Psalm 55:1-5 (KJV)
"Give ear to my prayer, O God; and hide not thyself from my supplication.
Attend unto me, and hear me: I mourn in my complaint, and make a noise;
Because of the voice of the enemy, because of the oppression of the wicked: for they cast iniquity upon me, and in wrath they hate me.
My heart is sore pained within me: and the terrors of death are fallen upon me.
Fearfulness and trembling are come upon me, and horror hath overwhelmed me."

Listen
In this Psalm, David writes about the troubles and terror that he faced in a season of his life. The troubles were from within and without, but they both drained him of his peace and his joy.

Psalm 55:6-8 (KJV)
"And I said, Oh that I had wings like a dove! *for then* would I fly away, and be at rest.
Lo, *then* would I wander far off, *and* remain in the wilderness. Selah.
I would hasten my escape from the windy storm *and* tempest."

When we find ourselves feeling like this, we often think, *"Will I ever get out of this pit?"* This is the time to be still, and remember who we are and whose we are. It is time to connect with our Father in Heaven.

Psalm 55:16-17 (KJV)
"As for me, I will call upon God; and the LORD shall save me. Evening, and morning, and at noon, will I pray, and cry aloud: and he shall hear my voice."

Yes, there is nothing in this world that will satisfy our souls and heal our wounded hearts like the presence of the Lord. That is why David writes this near the end of his Psalm, and you can claim this promise in your season of trouble and pain.

Psalm 55:22 (KJV)
"Cast thy burden upon the LORD, and he shall sustain thee: he shall never suffer the righteous to be moved."

The Apostle Peter drew upon this wisdom and wrote this encouragement to the first-century believers, and it still speaks to us today.

1 Peter 5:7 (KJV)
"Casting all your care upon him; for he careth for you."

Prayer
Father, I exalt and give praise and honor to Your name; the name that I cherish above every name on earth below and in Heaven above.

Father, hear our cry; hear our plea as we cry out to You in prayer for others and for ourselves. Father, we declare that our hope is in You and that our help comes from You.

Father, we know You can and You will hear our prayer. We watch and wait for Your answer to our prayers.

20
Abide

God Speaks
John 15:5 (KJV)
"I am the vine, ye *are* the branches: He that abideth in me, and I in him, the same bringeth forth much fruit: for without me ye can do nothing."

Listen
Do you want to be fruitful in your life? What is your mentality? Do you desire to be average or do you want to bear much fruit?

Pay attention to this word of Christ: "Whoever abides in me and I in him, he it is that bears much fruit." To abide in Christ is to follow, obey, and stay with Him.

Let's look into what the Word of God says about perseverance and preservation. Open your heart to receive this truth, by believing it in your heart and by obeying it with your whole heart. Remember, in everything, give God all of you, and receive from Him all of Him.

The Bible says about perseverance:
Romans 5:3-5 (NKJV)
"And not only *that,* but we also glory in tribulations, knowing that tribulation produces perseverance;
and perseverance, character; and character, hope.
Now hope does not disappoint, because the love of God has been poured out in our hearts by the Holy Spirit who was given to us."

Hebrews 10:36 (KJV)
"For ye have need of patience, that, after ye have done the will of God, ye might receive the promise."

Philippians 1:6 (KJV)
"Being confident of this very thing, that he which hath begun a good work in you will perform *it* until the day of Jesus Christ:"

The Bible says about preservation:

John 6:39 (KJV)
"And this is the Father's will which hath sent me, that of all which he hath given me I should lose nothing, but should raise it up again at the last day."

John 10:25-28 (KJV)
"Jesus answered them, I told you, and ye believed not: the works that I do in my Father's name, they bear witness of me.
But ye believe not, because ye are not of my sheep, as I said unto you. My sheep hear my voice, and I know them, and they follow me:
And I give unto them eternal life; and they shall never perish, neither shall any *man* pluck them out of my hand."

John 12:48 (KJV)
"He that rejecteth me, and receiveth not my words, hath one that judgeth him: the word that I have spoken, the same shall judge him in the last day."

One thing I have discovered about my reading of the Bible is that God does not have any grandchildren. You have to know God for yourself.

John 17:8 (KJV)
"For I have given unto them the words which thou gavest me; and they have received *them*, and have known surely that I came out from thee, and they have believed that thou didst send me."

Prayer
Father God, we are so grateful You can save and keep Your children.

> **Jude 1:24-25 (KJV)**
>
> "Now unto him that is able to keep you from falling, and to present *you* faultless before the presence of his glory with exceeding joy,
>
> To the only wise God our Saviour, *be* glory and majesty, dominion and power, both now and ever. Amen."

21
God's Presence

God Speaks
Psalm 105:4 (KJV)
"Seek the LORD, and his strength: seek his face evermore."

Listen
There is nowhere I would rather be than in the presence of the Lord. The verse above is my life's verse. It is the foundation for my mission statement, which is "Please God." We are never more pleasing to God than when we continually seek Him and live our lives in His presence.

The Bible says David was a man who pleased God. I have been reading the Psalms daily for many years and they have been an encouragement to me in my daily walk with the Lord. They have encouraged me to be a man who pleases God.

Read and reflect upon what David says about the presence of God and the priority David put on continually seeking the presence of the Lord.

Psalm 16:11 (KJV)
Thou wilt shew me the path of life: in thy presence *is* fullness of joy; at thy right hand *there are* pleasures for evermore.

Psalm 31:19-20 (KJV)
"*Oh* how great *is* thy goodness, which thou hast laid up for them that fear thee; *which* thou hast wrought for them that trust in thee before the sons of men!
Thou shalt hide them in the secret of thy presence from the pride of man: thou shalt keep them secretly in a pavilion from the strife of tongues."

Psalm 73:28 (KJV)
"But *it is* good for me to draw near to God: I have put my trust in the Lord GOD, that I may declare all thy works."

Psalm 73:24 (KJV)
"Thou shalt guide me with thy counsel, and afterward receive me *to* glory."

Prayer
Father God, Lord of lords, and King of kings, we pray for your continual and abiding presence in the hearts of Your children as we surrender our all to You, and receive all of You. Father, help each one of us to be pleasing to Your eyes.

22
What It Means to Be Chosen

God Speaks
1 Peter 2:9 (KJV)
"But ye *are* a chosen generation, a royal priesthood, an holy nation, a peculiar people; that ye should shew forth the praises of him who hath called you out of darkness into his marvellous light:"

Listen
How are you doing in being the person God redeemed you to be? When I read the above verse, I have to pause and meditate on it.

Listen to God as He speaks:
"But you are not like that, for you are a chosen people."

Who are you not like?

1 Peter 2:6-8 (KJV)
"Wherefore also it is contained in the scripture, Behold, I lay in Sion a chief corner stone, elect, precious: and he that believeth on him shall not be confounded.
Unto you therefore which believe *he is* precious: but unto them which be disobedient, the stone which the builders disallowed, the same is made the head of the corner,
And a stone of stumbling, and a rock of offence, *even to them* which stumble at the word, being disobedient: whereunto also they were appointed."

How are you doing in being a priest of God? Are you showing others the goodness of God? Are you taking the needs of others to God in prayer? Why not meditate on this Word of the Lord and allow the Holy Spirit to guide you in an evaluation of your faith and your faithfulness in being one of His chosen people.

1 Peter 2:1-3 (KJV)
"Wherefore laying aside all malice, and all guile, and hypocrisies, and envies, and all evil speakings,

As newborn babes, desire the sincere milk of the word, that ye may grow thereby:
If so be ye have tasted that the Lord *is* gracious."

Prayer
Our Father, help us, who are Your chosen people, to be royal priests by showing others the goodness of God, and bring the needs of others to your throne room of grace and mercy.

23

Are You Being Transformed?

God Speaks
Romans 12:1-2 (KJV)
"I beseech you therefore, brethren, by the mercies of God, that ye present your bodies a living sacrifice, holy, acceptable unto God, *which is* your reasonable service.
And be not conformed to this world: but be ye transformed by the renewing of your mind, that ye may prove what *is* that good, and acceptable, and perfect, will of God."

Listen
As I read the above passage, I am asking the Lord to search the depths of my heart and to reveal to me anything He sees that is not pleasing in His eyes. Are you willing to open the doors of every compartment of your life to the service of the Lord? Are you prepared to pray a prayer similar to this one?

Matthew 6:10 (KJV)
"Thy kingdom come. Thy will be done in earth, as *it is* in heaven."

My soul sings this Judson Van Deventer hymn:

> All to Jesus I surrender,
> All to Him I freely give;
> I will ever love and trust Him,
> In His presence daily live.
>
> I surrender all,
> I surrender all;
> All to Thee, my blessed Savior,
> I surrender all.

Are you willing to pray a prayer similar to this one? Let's unite our hearts in praying for one another.

Prayer
Father, I surrender my all to You in exchange for receiving all Your presence to rule and reign in my life. Father, I give You my life, by faith, so You can do your work of transforming me to be more and more like Jesus.

24
What Is God's Standard for His People?

God Speaks
1 Peter 1:15-16 (NKJV)
"but as He who called you *is* holy, you also be holy in all *your* conduct, because it is written, *"Be holy, for I am holy."* "

Listen
Is that standard too high? Peter quoted this Scripture in Leviticus 20:7 (NLT): "So set yourselves apart to be holy, for I am the Lord your God."

You need not fear or be afraid that you will not be able to meet the standard. You don't have to do it in your strength alone.

What God did for His servant, Mary, He will do for you.

Luke 1:49 (NKJV)
"For He who is mighty has done great things for me, And holy *is* His name."

Luke 1:37 (NKJV)
"For with God nothing will be impossible."

Prayer
Our Father, we need You every day if we are going to meet the standard of being holy in everything we do. Father, we thank you that the One who chose us and commands us to be holy is the One that will enable us to be holy like You are holy.

25
How Can I Ever Meet the Standard to Be Perfect?

God Speaks
Matthew 5:48 (KJV)
"Be ye therefore perfect, even as your Father which is in heaven is perfect."

Listen
Yes, Jesus said that in the Sermon on the Mount. As I meditate on this Scripture, I am comforted in knowing that what God expects of us He provides the means for us to accomplish as part of His purpose for our lives.

1 John 3:6 (KJV)
"Whosoever abideth in him sinneth not: whosoever sinneth hath not seen him, neither known him."

1 John 3:9 (KJV)
"Whosoever is born of God doth not commit sin; for his seed remaineth in him: and he cannot sin, because he is born of God."

Read the above verses often as you ponder the command to be perfect. The key is to surrender your whole heart to the Lord.

Matthew 5:48 (AMP)
"You, therefore, must be perfect [growing into complete maturity of godliness in mind and character, having reached the proper height of virtue and integrity], as your heavenly Father is perfect."

Finally, here is the enabling power to be perfect and pleasing in the eyes of our Father in Heaven.

Romans 5:3-5 (NKJV)
"And not only *that*, but we also glory in tribulations, knowing that tribulation produces perseverance;

and perseverance, character; and character, hope.
Now hope does not disappoint, because the love of God has been poured out in our hearts by the Holy Spirit who was given to us."

Prayer
Our Father, we thank you for giving us the Holy Spirit to fill our hearts with Your love so that we can be perfect as You are perfect.

Father, we long for the day when You will deliver Your people from the presence of sin.

26

Be Kind

God Speaks
Ephesians 4:30-32 (NKJV)
"And do not grieve the Holy Spirit of God, by whom you were sealed for the day of redemption.
Let all bitterness, wrath, anger, clamor, and evil speaking be put away from you, with all malice.
And be kind to one another, tenderhearted, forgiving one another, just as God in Christ forgave you."

Listen
We forfeit a divine opportunity to influence people because of lack of kindness. The Scripture speaks of things that the people of God should put off from their old life to become new creations in Christ Jesus.

2 Corinthians 5:17-18 (KJV)
"Therefore if any man *be* in Christ, *he is* a new creature: old things are passed away; behold, all things are become new.
And all things *are* of God, who hath reconciled us to himself by Jesus Christ, and hath given to us the ministry of reconciliation;"

When you put on Christ, you have a new nature, a new life, and a new purpose. These old habits grieve the Holy Spirit; they cause harm to the Body of Christ and invite Satan into your life to destroy your testimony.

Take action when you find yourself living according to the old life — your life before Christ came into your heart. Get rid of those things.

However, don't leave a vacuum. Take action with the enabling power of the Holy Spirit of God to live according to your new life in Christ Jesus.

Ephesians 4:32 (KJV)
"And be ye kind one to another, tenderhearted, forgiving one another, even as God for Christ's sake hath forgiven you."

Prayer
Our Father, we ask You would give us sufficient grace to be able to say yes to the Spirit of God and no to the desires of the world, the flesh, and the devil. Father, help us to be kind so that our lives and our words may bring praise and glory to the name of the Lord.

27
Be Thankful

God Speaks
Hebrews 12:28 (KJV)
"Wherefore we receiving a kingdom which cannot be moved, let us have grace, whereby we may serve God acceptably with reverence and godly fear:"

Listen
Our gratitude and our thankfulness should flow upward to God and horizontally to others as we come into contact with them on a daily basis.

Be grateful to God and give Him thanks.

Psalm 136:1 (KJV)
"O give thanks unto the LORD; for *he is* good: for his mercy *endureth* for ever."

Be grateful to others that you meet along life's journey in this fallen world that is our temporary dwelling place. This world is not our home.

Ephesians 1:16-17 (NLT)
"I have not stopped thanking God for you. I pray for you constantly, asking God, the glorious Father of our Lord Jesus Christ, to give you spiritual wisdom and insight so that you might grow in your knowledge of God."

Everything you have is a gift from God. It has been freely given to you. In the same manner, freely give to others.

James 1:17 (KJV)
"Every good gift and every perfect gift is from above, and cometh down from the Father of lights, with whom is no variableness, neither shadow of turning."

Prayer
Father God, by Your almighty power, we ask that You strengthen us to be our best and to give our best in service to You and others.

Philippians 1:6 (NLT)
"And I am certain that God, who began the good work within you, will continue his work until it is finally finished on the day when Christ Jesus returns."

28
Be Humble

God Speaks
Matthew 23:11-12 (KJV)
"But he that is greatest among you shall be your servant.
And whosoever shall exalt himself shall be abased; and he that shall humble himself shall be exalted."

Listen
The Lord does not look at His people the way the world looks at people nor by the way the world elevates people. The Lord looks at the heart.

Psalm 51:6 (KJV)
"Behold, thou desirest truth in the inward parts: and in the hidden *part* thou shalt make me to know wisdom."

Romans 12:3 (KJV)
"For I say, through the grace given unto me, to every man that is among you, not to think *of himself* more highly than he ought to think; but to think soberly, according as God hath dealt to every man the measure of faith."

When God says He is opposed to something, I take Him seriously. I don't want to find myself in the position of being for something that God disapproves.

James 4:6 (KJV)
"But he giveth more grace. Wherefore he saith, God resisteth the proud, but giveth grace unto the humble."

Prayer
Father God, I ask for sufficient grace to be humble, and to be a faithful servant of God and the people of God.

29

The Responsibility of the Hearer

God Speaks
Mark 4:24-25 (KJV)
"And he said unto them, Take heed what ye hear: with what measure ye mete, it shall be measured to you: and unto you that hear shall more be given.
For he that hath, to him shall be given: and he that hath not, from him shall be taken even that which he hath."

Listen
Jesus says in this discourse that the hearer has responsibility for what he hears and how he uses what he hears. Notice what else the Bible says about this important matter of how we handle the Word.

2 Timothy 2:15 (KJV)
"Study to shew thyself approved unto God, a workman that needeth not to be ashamed, rightly dividing the word of truth."

Acts 17:11 (NLT)
"And the people of Berea were more open-minded than those in Thessalonica, and they listened eagerly to Paul's message. They searched the Scriptures day after day to see if Paul and Silas were teaching the truth."

God has done, and He continues to do, His part. He has given us His Word to speak to us and the Holy Spirit to be our teacher and tutor.

1 John 2:26-27 (NLT)

> I am writing these things to warn you about those who want to lead you astray. But you have received the Holy Spirit, and he lives within you, so you don't need anyone to teach you what is true. For the Spirit teaches you everything you need to know, and what he teaches is true—it is not a lie. So just as he has taught you, remain in fellowship with Christ.

Mark 4:23 (NKJV)
"If anyone has ears to hear, let him hear."

Prayer
Our Father, we are so grateful You have given us the Word of God and the Holy Spirit to help and guide us to the way, the truth, and the eternal life You provide to all who receive Jesus.

Psalm 119:130 (AMP)
"The entrance and unfolding of your words give light; their unfolding gives understanding (discernment and comprehension) to the simple."

Father, we ask You would stir our hearts to have eyes that are open and ears that are eager to hear a word from You.

30

The Word of God

God Speaks
Isaiah 55:11 (KJV)
"So shall my word be that goeth forth out of my mouth: it shall not return unto me void, but it shall accomplish that which I please, and it shall prosper *in the thing* whereto I sent it."

Listen
I heard a message on the radio by Dr. Adrain Rodgers in which he gave these simple steps for meditating on a Bible passage. This six-step approach I have used for many years in reading the Bible devotionally.

1. Read it through.
2. Think it out.
3. Pray it in.
4. Write it down.
5. Live it out.
6. Pass it on.

Try reading this passage from Psalms, using the six-step approach listed above and listen to what God has to say to you.

Psalm 19:7-11 (NLT)

> The instructions of the Lord are perfect, reviving the soul. The decrees of the Lord are trustworthy, making wise the simple. The commandments of the Lord are right, bringing joy to the heart. The commands of the Lord are clear, giving insight for living. Reverence for the Lord is pure, lasting forever. The laws of the Lord are true; each one is fair. They are more desirable than gold, even the finest gold. They are sweeter than honey, even honey dripping from the comb. They

are a warning to your servant, a great reward for those who obey them.

The following acrostic says a lot in five words.

Basic
Instruction
Before
Leaving
Earth

Prayer
Father, we are so thankful that we have the Bible in a language we can read and understand. Father, we pray You would give us a hunger and thirst for the Bible.

Father, I pray many will be hearers and doers of the Word of God.

31
Prayer Is the Lifeblood of the Body of Christ

God Speaks
Matthew 7:7-8 (KJV)
"Ask, and it shall be given you; seek, and ye shall find; knock, and it shall be opened unto you:
For every one that asketh receiveth; and he that seeketh findeth; and to him that knocketh it shall be opened."

Listen
When you pray, it is a conversation between you and God. When I go to my place of prayer at home, I always have my Bible open as I read His Word. God speaks to me, I listen, and then I speak when it's my turn.

Listen to the words that the Apostle Paul writes to the church at Colossae, encouraging them to be devoted to prayer.

Colossians 4:2-5 (KJV)
"Continue in prayer, and watch in the same with thanksgiving;
Withal praying also for us, that God would open unto us a door of utterance, to speak the mystery of Christ, for which I am also in bonds:
That I may make it manifest, as I ought to speak.
Walk in wisdom toward them that are without, redeeming the time."

The key to an effective prayer life is to pray with a grateful heart. There are times when we need only to have just a little talk with the Lord. However, there are times when we need to have a big talk with the Lord. The lyrics of the Fanny Crosby hymn, "Draw Me Nearer", inform and inspire my prayer life.

> Oh, the pure delight of a single hour
> That before Thy throne I spend,
> When I kneel in prayer, and with Thee, my God
> I commune as friend with friend!

If Jesus had to pray, what about you and me?
Mark 1:35 (KJV)
"And in the morning, rising up a great while before day, he went out, and departed into a solitary place, and there prayed."

Prayer
Our Father, we pray that we, the Body of Christ, will be devoted to prayer. Father, give us the mind of Christ and the perseverance to continue in prayer. Father, give us sufficient faith, which is necessary to please You.

God is waiting to hear from you. Don't disappoint Him. Pray continuously, just like you breathe.

Psalm 116:2 (KJV)
"Because he hath inclined his ear unto me, therefore will I call upon *him* as long as I live."

Endorsement/Testimony

I have followed Herb Cotton's daily devotionals for many years. His devotionals make me feel that I have a close relationship with our Savior; giving me faith, hope, comfort, encouragement, peace, and answers to my everyday problems and tribulations.

For me, it is a most necessary reading to understand God's words and will. Herb Cotton is truly a man after God's Scripture. I look forward to the release of his first book, *31 Days of Hearing God Speak*.

Yolanda Polanco
Mesa, Arizona

Herbert Cotton's Life, A Prayerful Journey

During my twenty-five years of being a pastor in Anchorage, it has been my blessing to pray with, for, and in unity with Herbert Cotton. I have observed that he is a man of effective prayer. This thirty-one-day devotional is a refinement and remembrance of his devotion to prayer! His pleasing baritone voice proclaiming "that prayer is the lifeblood of the church;" the airways coming alive with the intercession and comfort given on his radio program "Praying for You." I was a guest on his program many times.

Entwined within these thirty-one devotionals are Herbert's witness and testimony of the biblical expression of divine communication!

May these thirty-one devotionals encourage and exhort on your prayerful journey.

Charles Johnston
Pastor, Hope Christian Fellowship
Anchorage, Alaska

Testimony of Herb Cotton's Daily Devotionals

As life allows storms in our life, we need to be like the tree that is rooted in the Lord near a stream, roots deep in His Word. Knowing that the storms will come and the winds will blow yet we will be strong because we can withstand anything because Christ is always with us. Herb has been obedient to God's call and sharing what God has said to him in his daily devotionals. May these words give you all you need for today and for many years to come. I look forward to seeing how this book speaks to both your heart and mine. God is calling us to pray and may you find time each day to just rejoice in all He has done for you this day.

Lisa Moore

www.ingramcontent.com/pod-product-compliance
Ingram Content Group UK Ltd.
Pitfield, Milton Keynes, MK11 3LW, UK
UKHW041956230426
12048UKWH00008B/370